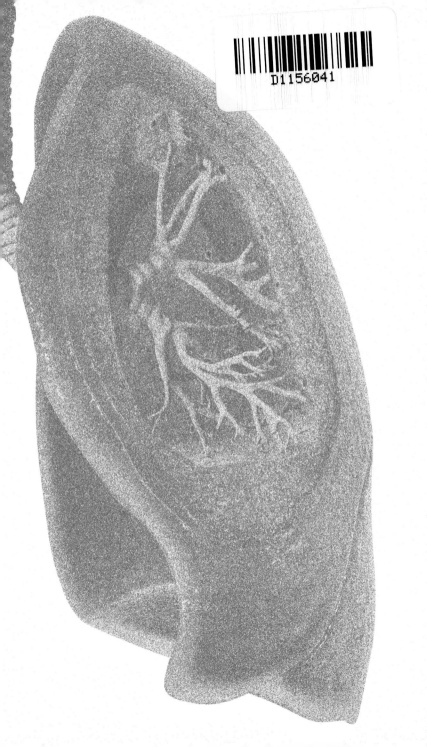

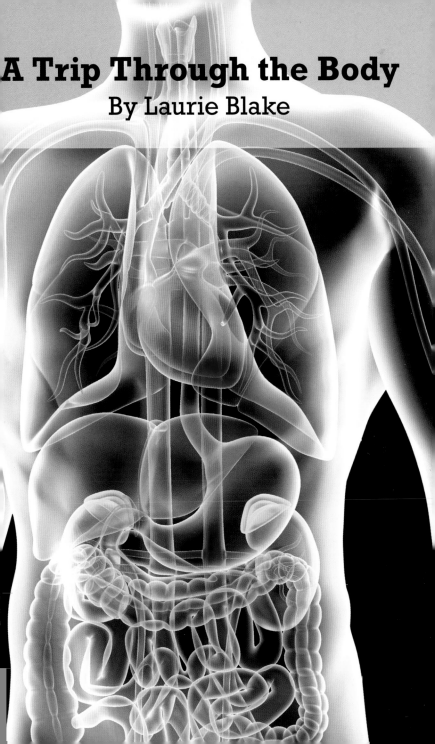

A Trip Through the Body
By Laurie Blake

Series Editor Deborah Lock
US Senior Editor Shannon Beatty
Project Editor Katy Lennon
Editor Nandini Gupta
Senior Art Editor Ann Cannings
Art Editor Yamini Panwar
Managing Editor Soma B. Chowdhury
Managing Art Editor Ahlawat Gunjan
Art Director Martin Wilson
Senior Producer, Pre-production Ben Marcus
Senior DTP Designer Neeraj Bhatia
DTP Designer Anita Yadav
Picture Researcher Sumedha Chopra

Reading Consultant Dr. Linda Gambrell, Ph.D.

Subject Consultant Steve Parker

First American Edition, 2015
Published in the United States by DK Publishing
345 Hudson Street, New York, New York 10014

A catalog record for this book is available from the Library of Congress.
ISBN: 978-1-4654-2933-9 (paperback)
ISBN: 978-1-4654-2932-2 (hardback)

DK books are available at special discounts when purchased
in bulk for sales promotions, premiums, fund-raising, or
educational use. For details, contact: DK Publishing Special
Markets, 345 Hudson Street, New York, New York 10014
or SpecialSales@dk.com.
Printed and bound in China

· ·A WORLD OF IDEAS: ··· · · ·
SEE ALL THERE IS TO KNOW ·

Contents

Body Mechanics

From our heads to our toes, our bodies are the most complex and the most amazing machines.

No computer can match our brains for creativity and problem-solving ability.

Our eyes can focus more accurately than a video camera.

We don't just make sounds to communicate like a radio, but we can also change expressions and use body language.

Our lungs don't just pump air in and out but can extract oxygen from air, too.

We're even better at adapting our movements than an "all-terrain" vehicle. We can walk, run, or climb almost anywhere.

Our digestive system is better than a food processor, since we don't just mash our food. Our intestines break it down into useful chemicals for energy.

No toolbox is needed since we have living cells that can self-repair and heal our bodies.

We're better than fans in an oven and a refrigerator combined, since we can not only heat up our bodies but also cool them down.

No identical copies can be made, since our bodies are unique to each one of us, but we can pass on characteristics to our children.

Our bodies have a lifetime guarantee!

Think of a machine and consider how your body can do the same and more!

Prologue
Looking Inside

The inside story of the human body is exciting, gruesome, and even entertaining. Over many centuries, doctors, scientists, and others have been fascinated by what our bodies are made of and how they work. Thanks to their efforts, they've pieced together facts so that we now understand the human body's systems and the roles each part of the body plays. The research continues because there is so much more to explore and find out.

Each bit of the body is made from microscopic living cells. This was discovered by Dutchman Antoni van Leeuwenhoek in the 1600s when he designed a simple microscope. Altogether, there are about 200 different types of cells, including blood cells, bone cells, and brain cells. Cells with the same task work together to make tissues, such as muscles. Different types of tissues cooperate to form organs, like the stomach or brain. Organs with linked roles make up a system. Altogether, 12 systems fit together to make up the workings of our bodies.

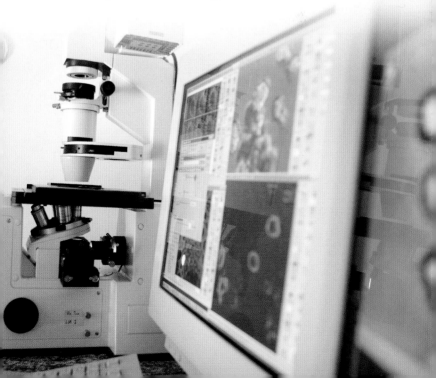

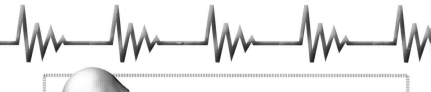

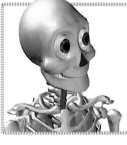

?

Name three ways that doctors today can see inside the human body.

Until the end of the 19th century, the best way that doctors could see inside the body—living or dead—was to cut it open. This changed in 1895 when German scientist Wilhelm Roentgen found that X-rays could pass through soft things, like skin and muscle, but showed the hard parts, like bones. By projecting X-rays through the body onto photographic film, Roentgen could produce a picture of the inside of the body showing just the bones. Doctors could now see fractures and weird things like bullets and swallowed coins.

More high-tech methods were invented during the 1970s–1980s. One of them, called MRI (magnetic resonance imaging), combines magnetism and radio waves to produce images of "slices" through the body. Another method called ultrasound bounces sound waves off body parts and uses the echo to make a picture of what's happening inside. Ultrasound is safe to use to check how a baby is growing inside its mother.

Finding a way of examining the body's insides and seeing into its organs has been an aim of medical researchers. This procedure is called endoscopy. In 1806, Philipp Bozzini introduced his "Lichtleiter" to study the hollow organs and body cavities. This device had a light source, a part for inserting into the body, and mirrors to project the image.

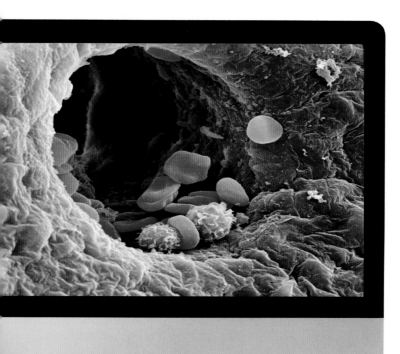

Over the next two centuries, many improvements were made that enabled surgeons to see what they were doing while operating inside parts of the body. In 1956, French researchers used a device with video cameras, and since the 1970s, relaying digital images has been possible. Today the quickly received images are clearer and magnified to a larger size.

The way ahead is by using wireless endoscopy. Capsules have been made that when swallowed by the patient then open up to become a camera, relaying images once inside the body. In the future, devices will certainly become even smaller and maybe even small remote-controlled robots could treat a patient from within the body.

At the moment, the devices are not small enough to travel through every part of the body, but this could become possible one day in the future.

Build a Body

Here's a list of the many parts that make up the human body. Each part works with other parts to get the body's systems working together. They are all packed tightly together to fit.

Parts list

- ☑ **206** bones
- ☑ **640** muscles
- ☑ **10** pints of blood
- ☑ **32** teeth
- ☑ 1 tongue
- ☑ **5** million hairs
- ☑ **20** keratin nails
- ☑ 1 bag of skin
- ☑ 1 heart
- ☑ 2 lungs
- ☑ 2 lips
- ☑ 2 eyeballs
- ☑ 1 nose

- ☑ **2** outer earflaps
- ☑ **2** inner ears
- ☑ 1 food tube
- ☑ 1 windpipe
- ☑ 1 voice box
- ☑ 1 stomach
- ☑ 1 small intestine
- ☑ 1 large intestine
- ☑ 1 anus
- ☑ 2 kidneys
- ☑ 1 bladder
- ☑ 1 gallbladder
- ☑ 1 liver…

Position guide

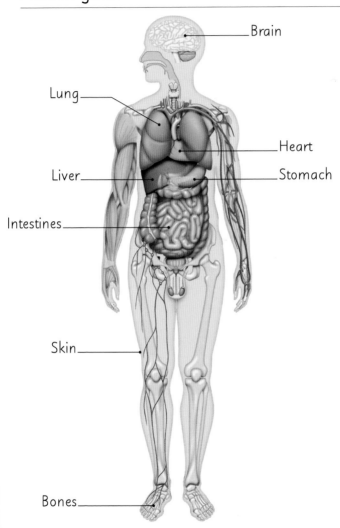

Brain

Lung

Heart

Liver

Stomach

Intestines

Skin

Bones

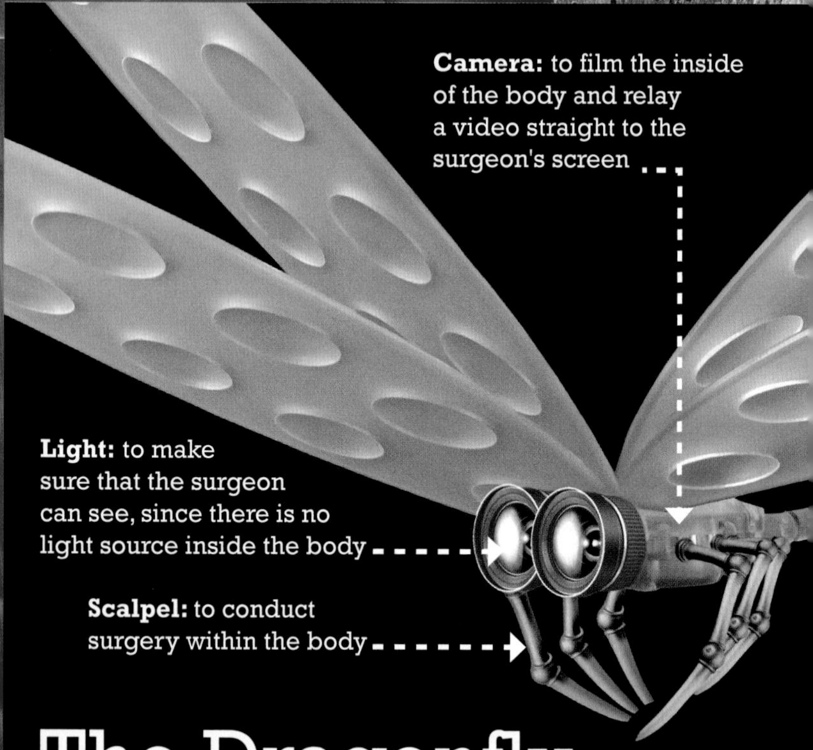

Camera: to film the inside of the body and relay a video straight to the surgeon's screen

Light: to make sure that the surgeon can see, since there is no light source inside the body

Scalpel: to conduct surgery within the body

The Dragonfly

Here is an imaginary wireless microscopic remote-controlled device that could be used for exploring inside a human body. The diagram shows the features that an endoscopy device of the future would need.

Wings: to help control the direction that the device is moving

Motor: to propel the device through the body and to control the speed at which it moves

Endoscopy

An endoscopy procedure is the term used for when a doctor explores the inside of the human body. Doctors commonly use a small camera, attached to a tube, which is inserted into a natural opening in the body, for example the mouth or nose. It can also be inserted into the body through a small surgical cut made in the skin. Endoscopes can only investigate hollow organs or cavities in the body because they are too big to fit anywhere else.

Latest Discoveries

The Nobel Prize for physiology or medicine in 2014 has been awarded to three scientists that discovered the brain's "GPS system."

Professors John O'Keefe, May-Britt Moser, and Edvard Moser share the award. They discovered how the brain knows where we are and is able to navigate from one place to another.

On hearing about winning the prize, Professor O'Keefe from University College London, UK, said, "I'm totally delighted and thrilled. I'm still in a state of shock. It's the highest accolade you can get."

O'Keefe first described how a set of nerve cells formed a map within the brain in the early 1970s, but at that time people scoffed at the idea. However, as a fellow professor commented, "Now, like so many ideas that were at first highly controversial, people say 'Well that's obvious!'"

Previous winners of the Nobel Prize for physiology or medicine include James Rothman, Randy Schekman, and Thomas Südhof in 2013 for their discovery of how cells precisely transport material. Bruce Beutler, Jules Hoffmann, and Ralph Steinman in 2011 won the prize after revolutionizing the understanding of how the body fights infection.

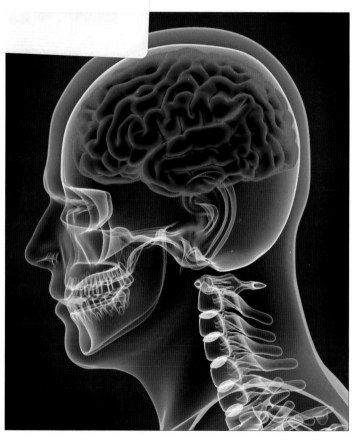

The Nobel Prize for physiology or medicine has been awarded 105 times to 207 Nobel Laureates between 1901 and 2014.

Chapter 1
Cruising the Circulatory System

Our bodies are made of trillions of cells, and each one requires a nonstop supply of food, oxygen, and other goodies. In order to get this, the heart pumps blood around the body through blood vessels. This is known as the circulatory system.

Red and runny, blood contains billions of cells floating in a liquid called plasma. This blood plasma is mainly water, but has more than a hundred different chemicals dissolved in it, including different types of food.

The plasma travels through a massive network of blood vessels, carrying blood on a round trip to every nook and cranny of the body. This network of veins, arteries, and capillaries functions much like a conveyor belt. The red blood cells absorb oxygen that the other cells need and pass it along. These dimpled deliverers are packed with an orangey-red substance called hemoglobin that loads up with oxygen. However, when you see blood normally, the blood cells are so small that we can't see them individually, so it looks like the liquid is red. When the blood arrives in the big toe, earlobe, and every other part of the body, the hemoglobin unloads its oxygen to satisfy demands.

There are around five million red blood cells in just one milliliter of blood, and the human body has around ten pints of blood inside at any one time. So, really, we're likely to have around twenty-five trillion red blood cells traveling around our bodies.

These red, floating, disklike objects rush on in a seemingly endless stream, flooding along the tubular network. Each tube is made up of hundreds of tiny segments.

Arteries carry blood away from the heart under high pressure. Luckily, artery walls are both strong and elastic. With each powerful heartbeat surge, the walls bulge outward and then spring back. Where an artery comes near the skin's surface, we can feel this bouncing action.

Arteries branch all over the body, eventually leading into microscopic vessels called capillaries. These capillaries are so small that red blood cells sometimes have to bend sideways to fit inside them. Capillaries pass right by cells so that food and oxygen can pass from the blood and into the cells.

Job done! The capillaries link up to form veins that carry the blood back to the heart. Veins have thinner walls and the blood travels along them with far less pressure. Valves stop blood from flowing backward. Veins take blood back to the heart to begin another trip around the circulatory system.

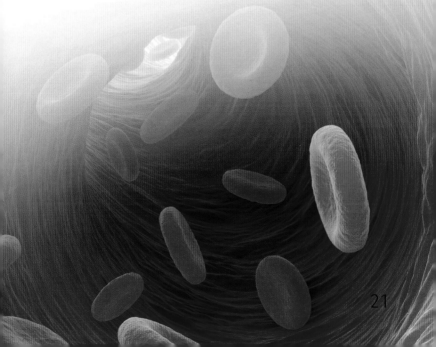

Every person belongs to one of four blood groups, which are dependent on the type of red blood cells we have. The types are called A, B, AB, and O. Only the matching blood type can be transferred into a patient who has lost blood. Before doctors knew this, if people were given the

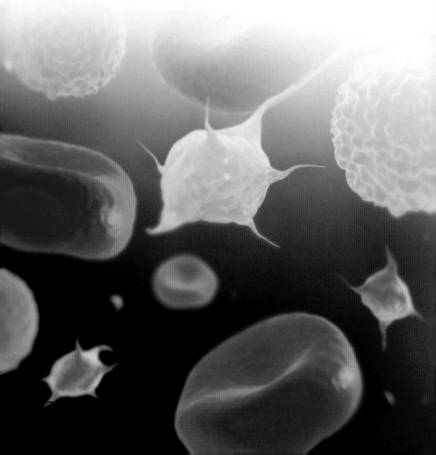

wrong type of blood, their red blood cells would stick together and the small blood vessels became blocked and prevented the circulatory system from working. Thankfully, millions of safe blood transfusions now take place every day.

There are more than red cells in blood though. White blood cells are like the police of our bodies. They patrol the bloodstream looking for anything that doesn't belong or could make us sick, and then they eat them. They hunt and kill invading germs before they cause trouble.

Also drifting aimlessly along in the blood are a selection of much smaller, pale cells dotted throughout. These are platelets and provide a 24-hour repair service to the body. They help stop bleeding and keep the blood in the tubes.

Whenever we get a cut or damage a blood vessel, the platelets join together in the thousands and seal it off completely. Their tiny tendrils grow out, reaching out toward the hole. Then their tendrils grab onto the edges of the tear, attaching themselves to one another until they completely seal it off. A scab forms over the plug to help the cut heal. Ingenious!

To do its job, blood needs to be pumped around the body. This is the task of the heart. The oxygen-poor blood enters from large veins that open out into a chamber called the right atrium. This cavity repeatedly compresses and expands, which sends the blood into the right ventricle, and then on to the lungs. As blood exits, so the heart refills over and over every beat.

To a tiny blood cell, the heart seems gigantic but this is only half of it. The right side sends blood into the lungs to collect oxygen, while the left side pumps it out again and through the body. The heart does this one, single function, but it's one of the most important organs in the entire body!

As we sit and read, our hearts are probably beating about 70 times each minute. A built-in pacemaker keeps the heart beating at the right rate. With each beat, flappy heart valves close to stop blood from going in the wrong direction. This makes the thumping sounds we hear if we listen to someone's chest.

The heart beats even faster when we're running, which means it sends blood around the system even faster. The blood can then get to where it's needed, especially to the muscles, very quickly. The circulatory system adjusts itself in many ways depending on how we're feeling or what we're doing so that we get just what we need at the rate we need it. It's very precise.

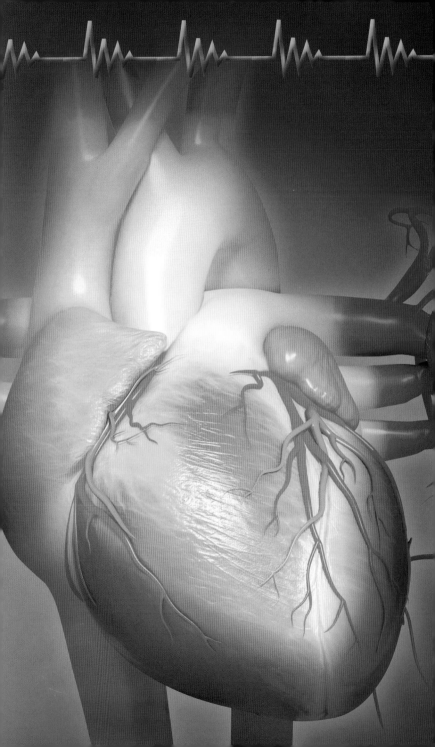

Blood Cell
QUICK FACTS

Red blood cells have a life span of 120 days. Two million new red blood cells are made by bone marrow every second.

Blood makes up about 7 percent of your body's weight.

During its life, a red blood cell will travel over 300 miles (480 km) and go through the heart 170,000 times. That's about one trip through the heart every minute.

A pinhead-sized drop of blood contains 5 million red blood cells, 7,000 white blood cells, and 300,000 platelets.

Red blood cells contain hemoglobin, a red-colored protein that carries oxygen. A single cell contains 250 million hemoglobin molecules.

One pint (500 ml) of donated blood can save up to three lives.

Blood cannot be manufactured—it can only come from generous donors.

Blood plasma transports dissolved substances around the body. These include nutrients, waste products, and hormones.

It would take 1,200,000 mosquitoes, each sucking once, to completely drain the average human body of blood.

There are around 60,000 miles (96,560 km) of blood vessels in an adult human body. That's enough to stretch around the world twice!

The heart can continue to beat when separated from the body, as long as it has a supply of oxygen.

Pump it **Up**!

This diagram shows the heart—where blood comes from and where it is pumped to.

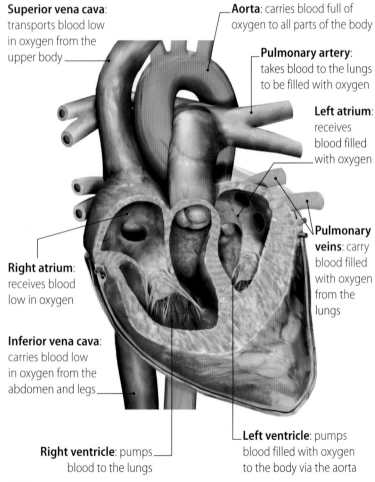

Superior vena cava: transports blood low in oxygen from the upper body

Aorta: carries blood full of oxygen to all parts of the body

Pulmonary artery: takes blood to the lungs to be filled with oxygen

Left atrium: receives blood filled with oxygen

Pulmonary veins: carry blood filled with oxygen from the lungs

Right atrium: receives blood low in oxygen

Inferior vena cava: carries blood low in oxygen from the abdomen and legs

Right ventricle: pumps blood to the lungs

Left ventricle: pumps blood filled with oxygen to the body via the aorta

What happens during a heartbeat:

The human heart works hard to pump blood to all parts of the body. Each heartbeat is made up of precisely timed muscle contractions that squeeze blood in and out of the heart's chambers.

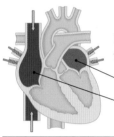

1 The heart's muscular wall is relaxed as blood from the lungs and body flows into the left and right atria.

Left atrium fills with blood full of oxygen

Right atrium fills with blood low in oxygen

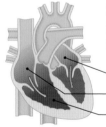

2 The left and right atria contract together, forcing blood through the valves and into the ventricles.

Atria muscles contract

Valves between the atria and ventricles open

Ventricles fill with blood

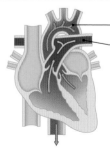

Blood pumped to the body

Blood pumped to the lungs

3 The two ventricles contract together, pushing blood to the lungs and body. Valves prevent blood from moving in the wrong direction.

Chapter 2
Riding the Respiratory System

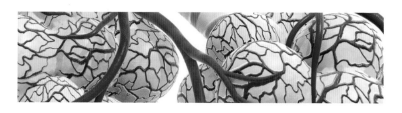

At this very moment, the cells in our bodies are using up oxygen. Why? To release energy stored in them from the food eaten in recent meals. This energy powers the activities that keep our cells alive, and also keep our bodies warm. Carbon dioxide is produced as a waste.

Earth's atmosphere contains the oxygen we need. Taking in oxygen and getting rid of carbon dioxide through breathing in and out is the main role of the respiratory system. We can't live without it!

For this important process to happen, our bodies have to breathe air into our left and right lungs. These are in the space inside our chests protected by the ribcage. Two muscles help the body breathe: the diaphragm, a big sheet of muscle just below the lungs, and the rib muscles. As we breathe in, the ribs move up, the diaphragm moves down, and the space inside the chest enlarges, sucking air into the lungs. When the muscles relax, the space reduces, squeezing the air out of the lungs. This automatically happens even when we're asleep. The brain keeps us breathing in and out between 12 and 18 times a minute when we're not doing much.

?

Why do the cells in our bodies need a constant supply of oxygen?

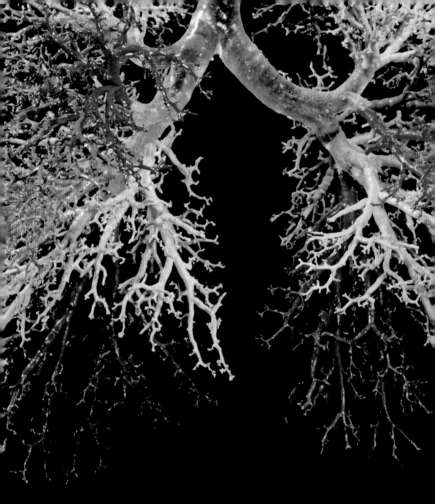

The soft, spongy lungs are a great
space far bigger than the heart, but filled
with a huge spread of treelike spindles,
crisscrossing throughout the entire area.
This amazing sight is known as the
bronchial tree.

The tiniest tubes called the bronchioles end in microscopic air bags with very thin walls called alveoli. If spread out, alveoli would cover one-third of a tennis court.

Twisted around each of these alveoli are the blood vessels that are filled with the oxygen-poor blood pumped from the heart. This is where the gas exchange takes place. As we breathe in, each branch fills with air so that the red blood cells can absorb the oxygen and carry it around the body. The carbon dioxide carried in the blood goes in the opposite direction into the air inside the alveoli, ready to be ejected out of the body in the next breath out.

We breathe in air through our mouth and nose and like a tremendous wind, the air is buffeted down the windpipe and into the lungs at the speed of a hurricane. It gets warm and damp on its journey. We take in about one pint of air with each breath. If we breathe in deeply, we can take in about six pints in one gulp.

Inside the airways is just for air, and the body wants to keep it as clear as possible so that we can breathe. However, when we breathe in, we pull a lot more than just air into us. Dust, bacteria, and other microscopic things get sucked down. That's where those white blood cells come in, making sure none of them survive in the blood.

When someone has asthma, they're allergic to something microscopic in the air. When they breathe it in, the body realizes how dangerous it is and fights to keep it out. But unfortunately it does this by squeezing shut these windpipes, which makes it much harder to breathe clearly. Our bodies will always try to protect us, even if we don't know what is happening or why.

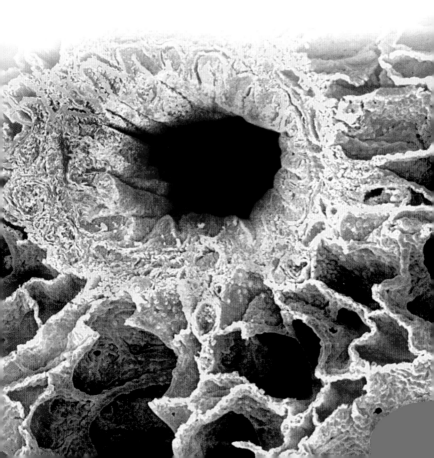

All that breathed-in air could also damage the delicate parts of the lungs, so the nose has a built-in filter system. The sticky mucus layer inside traps tiny pieces of dust. A nose irritation from dust or a cold virus triggers an automatic reflex action—a sneeze! Sneezing rapidly clears the nose, sending out droplets of watery mucus at speeds that can reach 100 miles per hour.

Coughs are another automatic reflex to blow out dust and other irritations from the airways. The lower part of the main windpipe closes so that air pressure builds up in the lungs, and then is released with an explosive force.

The rattling noise of a cough is made by the air rapidly passing the vocal cords on its way out. The vocal cords are two strands stretched across the top of the main airway. They are found in the voice box, which is the bumpy bit that can be felt at the front of the neck. The air rushing up from the lungs makes the two closed cords vibrate and produce sounds. The shape of the tongue, cheeks, and lips turn these sounds into understandable words to speak and sing. The harder the air is forced out of the lungs, the louder the sound.

Sometimes, when people sleep, the fleshy parts at the back of the nose and throat also vibrate as they breathe. Snore!

Respiratory System

Breathing is an automatic process—we don't really think about doing it. Yet it is vital to our survival. Our body cells need a continual supply of oxygen to work. The air around us contains this oxygen.

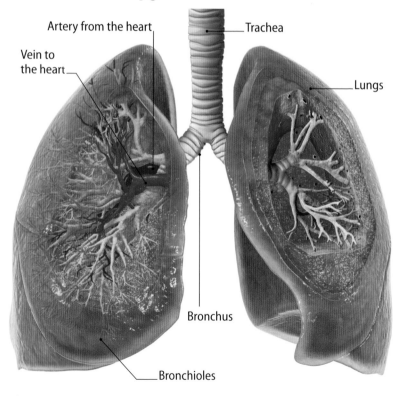

Artery from the heart

Trachea

Vein to the heart

Lungs

Bronchus

Bronchioles

Every incoming breath brings a new supply of oxygen deep into our lungs. Our body processes produce carbon dioxide. Every outgoing breath removes this.

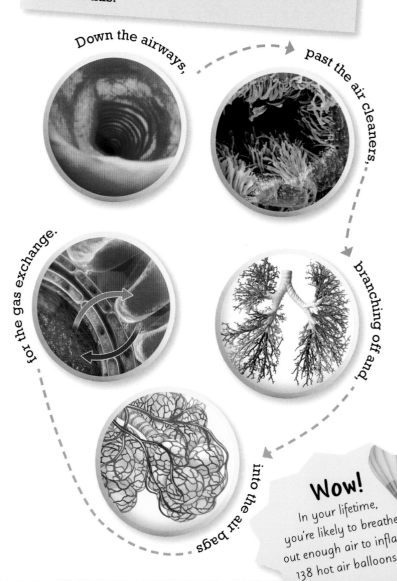

Down the airways,

past the air cleaners,

branching off and,

into the air bags

for the gas exchange.

Wow!

In your lifetime, you're likely to breathe out enough air to inflate 138 hot air balloons.

Take a Deep Breath!

STRIKE A CHORD SINGING SCHOOL

Welcome, boys and girls, to your first vocal training session with me, Ms. Harmony. Today we are going to learn how to control our breath in order to make the most of our beautiful singing voices!

Breath control is the most important part of singing—it allows us to sing through long phrases and also control the volume and pitch of our voices. In order to get air into our lungs, a muscle called the diaphragm (which is located just below the ribcage) contracts to increase space in the chest cavity. This space can then be filled with air. In order to exhale, the diaphragm relaxes and this pushes air back out of the lungs. As air is on its way out of the body, it has to pass the vocal cords, which vibrate and create sound.

Let's try these simple breathing exercises to see how well you can master the art of breathing!

1 Lie on the floor on your back and put a book on your stomach. Breathe in and out slowly. You should see the book rising and falling as you breathe. You need to concentrate on relaxing your tummy muscles when you breathe in and then tightening them in order to push out as much air as possible.

2 Breathe in for 4 seconds, hold your breath for 4 seconds, and then breathe out for 4 seconds. Once you can do this with ease, slowly increase the time by one second and then keep going until you can reach 10 seconds. This exercise will help you control the movements of your diaphragm.

3 Take a deep breath and when you exhale make a hissing sound. Keep this sound going for as long as you can. Keep practicing this and try to keep the noise going for a little bit longer each time. Try to make sure that the hissing is consistent, so not louder at the beginning and quieter at the end. You are aiming for a smooth and even sound.

Breathing Investigation

An experiment to test the effects of exercise on breathing.

You will need:

2 people

stopwatch

paper and pencil

jump rope

Hypothesis
A person's breathing will become faster with exercise.

Method

One person uses the stopwatch to time a minute for each activity and count the number of breaths. One breath is breathing in and then out again.

The other person does each of the following activities for one minute. Make sure that breathing becomes normal again before starting the next activity.

Results

Draw a chart like this and record the number of breaths taken during each activity.

	Name	Name
Sitting		
Walking in place		
Running in place		
Jumping		
Skipping		

Conclusion

The more active the exercise, the harder and faster a person breathes.

Explanation

Most people breathe in about 10–20 times each minute. However, during an activity, the busy muscles need more oxygen, so we have to breathe harder and faster to take in more oxygen.

Chapter 3
Diving Down the Digestive System

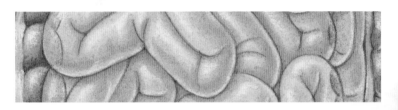

Running, talking, even sitting still are all activities that need energy. That energy comes from food. The body processes the food we eat, breaking it down, releasing all the vital nutrients we need to keep alive and healthy. All this is processed in the digestive system.

The first stage is to get the food inside our bodies. We're not like pythons that can swallow their food in one big lump. Instead, we use our toothy tool kit to chop up food into pieces small enough to be swallowed. While the jaws are chomping, salivary glands squirt juicy saliva into the mixture and the tongue mixes it all up. Usually, lips close to keep the food from falling out, and to avoid showing the whole chewing process going on in someone else's mouth!

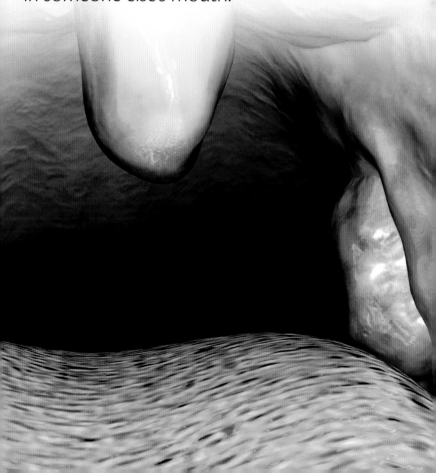

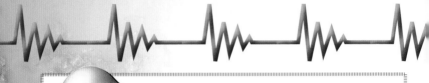

?

What stops the food from going the wrong way?

There are four types of teeth that chomp the food as if in a food processor. Chisel-like incisors cut the food and pointed canines grip it. The flat-topped premolars along either side and the large molars at the back grind the food. Young children have 20 milk teeth, which are then pushed out as they are replaced with 32 permanent teeth. Teeth are covered in a hard substance called enamel that is able to resist the wear and tear caused by chewing. However, sticky plaque, a mixture of food and bacteria, may build up if teeth are not cleaned. The bacteria release acids that can damage the hard enamel and cause tooth decay.

Everywhere in the digestive system, thick, slimy mucus makes it easy for food to slip along the tubes. Mucus is certainly important when it comes to swallowing. Once food has been chewed into a squishy ball, the tongue pushes it backward. The second it hits the throat, it is automatically swallowed.

The only thing that stops the food from going the wrong way is the epiglottis— a piece of tissue that keeps the air going into the air pipe and food into the food pipe. On a wave of muscle squeezes, food is pushed down the tube called the esophagus like a waterslide. The lining of the esophagus is covered with tiny folds, which trap the slimy mucus, making it easier for food to flow down. The muscles in the esophagus work so well that we'd still be able to swallow even if we were standing on our heads.

Like toothpaste being squeezed out of a tube, food arrives in the stomach and plunges into a large lake of hissing, bubbling, acidic juice. This juice partly digests it and kills off most nasty bacteria. The chewed-up food is also pulverized by the crushing motion of the stomach's muscular wall, turning into a soupy slop.

The stomach wall is very stretchy so that it can expand to hold big meals. Glands in the wall make and squirt out the acidic juice that starts digesting the food. The stomach

produces up to six pints of gastric juices every day.

After about four hours in the stomach, most food is gloopy enough to move on to the next stage. Greasy fatty foods take longer and rich food can spend twice as long in here.

Once the food breaks down, the stomach flushes the remains into the intestines. The muscle around the hole at the bottom of the stomach squeezes tightly closed once it passes through.

There are two parts to the intestines: the small and the large. The small intestine is actually the longest bit of the digestive system, but it's much narrower than the large intestine and so it is called "small." If the small intestine wasn't coiled up inside us, we would have to be a towering 21 feet tall for it to fit.

When the soupy food arrives from the stomach, it is bombarded with digestive juices again. These juices contain lots of chemical digesters called enzymes that break food down into small useful bits for the body's cells.

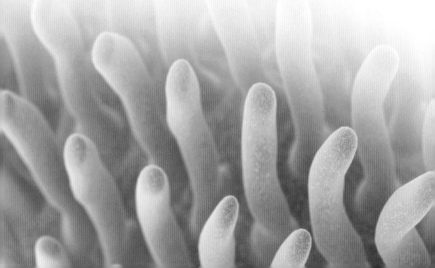

Throughout the small intestine, tiny fingerlike feelers stick out of the wall. These are called villi, and each one is connected to the bloodstream. As food that's been broken down by the acid swirls past, these villi soak up the nutrients and transfer it directly to the blood ready for speedy distribution to body cells.

The food slop continues being squeezed along and enters the large intestine. Where the small and large intestines meet there is a sudden change. The lining of the small intestine is folded so it can absorb digested food. The lining of the large intestine is flatter and covered in slimy mucus.

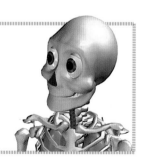

?

Why do the nutrients from the food need to go into the bloodstream?

In the large intestines, the food really changes. Feces, the brown bits that come out when we go to the toilet, are formed in this section. The main part of the large intestines is called the colon. It's about five feet long and starts near the appendix and stretches up, across, and down.

The slop dries out, as the much-needed water is absorbed back into the blood. The slimy mucus helps the dry feces slide along easily. Feces are being constantly churned and mixed, propelled along by the small wave movement of the muscles.

The thick layer of "friendly" bacteria lining the large intestine breaks down any food remains to release gases that make farts. These bacteria also make the substances that give feces their smell, and the brown stuff that gives feces their color.

Between 24 and 48 hours after swallowing a meal, squashy feces arrive in the rectum at the end of the colon. A message from here to the brain tells us that it's time to visit the toilet.

Stomach Acid Analysis

Here are some questions and answers about the inner workings of the stomach.

What is seen under the microscope?

You are looking at the microscopic view of the stomach's lining. It shows openings to some glands. When food enters the stomach, the glands release **gastric juice**. The movements of the stomach's muscular wall churn the food and juice around.

What are the components of gastric juice?

It's a feisty mix! There are enzymes called **proteases** and an acid mainly composed of **hydrochloric acid**, potassium, and sodium.

What do the proteases do?

They are bond-breakers! The **proteases** break down (digest) all the proteins in the food. They break the chemical bonds in proteins to free the chemicals (amino acids) needed by the body. **Proteases** work best in acid. After three to four hours, the food and juice becomes a creamy liquid.

Isn't hydrochloric acid very strong?

Yes, that's right. The **hydrochloric acid** is stronger than lemon juice. Outside the body, it can strip paint or eat right through a piece of wood. Inside your stomach, it makes conditions so harsh that dangerous bacteria on the food can't survive.

Why doesn't the acid eat the stomach too?

It's protected! The stomach is lined with mucus and some other glands release sodium bicarbonate. Bicarbonate is an alkali, which balances the acid, producing harmless salt and water.

Wow!

During an average lifetime, a person can eat and digest up to 50 tons of food and release about 4–6 pints of gastric juice every day.

The Journey of Food ┄┄┐

Join your food guide on an amazing two-day trip through the human digestive system. This rollercoaster tour will let you experience first-hand what happens to food after it has been eaten. An absorbing travel experience for any morsel!

Terms and conditions

Journey times may vary (between 20 and 48 hours) depending on the type of food being digested.

ITINERARY

00:00:00
Arrival in the mouth where food will be gnashed by teeth and mushed up with saliva.

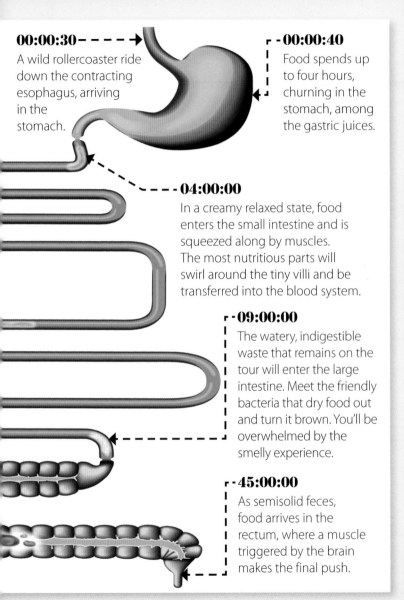

00:00:30
A wild rollercoaster ride down the contracting esophagus, arriving in the stomach.

00:00:40
Food spends up to four hours, churning in the stomach, among the gastric juices.

04:00:00
In a creamy relaxed state, food enters the small intestine and is squeezed along by muscles. The most nutritious parts will swirl around the tiny villi and be transferred into the blood system.

09:00:00
The watery, indigestible waste that remains on the tour will enter the large intestine. Meet the friendly bacteria that dry food out and turn it brown. You'll be overwhelmed by the smelly experience.

45:00:00
As semisolid feces, food arrives in the rectum, where a muscle triggered by the brain makes the final push.

The Scoop on **Poop!**

All animals **poop**, but waste products differ depending on what the animal eats.

Herring gull

Diet: gulls hunt for fish and other sea creatures and also eat eggs, worms, and other small mammals.

Shape of dung: herring gulls' feces are usually excreted as liquid, but they have a delicate digestive system so they need to regurgitate, or "throw up," food that they are unable to digest.

Interesting fact: some people believe that it is "good luck" to be pooped on by a bird.

Rabbit

Diet: all rabbits are herbivores and survive on grass, flowers, and weeds.

Shape of dung: rabbits have two types of droppings: some are small hard pellets, and others are soft black pellets.

Interesting fact: rabbits struggle to digest all of the plants that they eat so they eat their soft pellets, digesting their food further and taking in extra nutrients.

Here is an idea of what different animal dung is like—from very big animals to very small ones.

Elephant

Diet: elephants are herbivores and their diet consists of grass, leaves, bark, twigs, and fruit.

Shape of dung: elephant dung is large and round and full of undigested grass.

Interesting fact: elephant dung can be used to make paper because it is very fibrous. This is a great alternative to paper made from trees because it is a natural and plentiful resource.

Human

Diet: most humans have a varied diet that needs to include a healthy balance of carbohydrates, fats, proteins, vitamins, minerals, fiber, and water.

Shape of dung: human feces vary from person to person since everyone has a different diet.

Interesting fact: humans create a new stomach lining every three to four days. If they didn't, the strong acids their stomach uses to digest food would also digest their stomach.

Chapter 4
Intercepted by the Immune System

Germs or bugs are always hanging around, trying to get inside our bodies. Those that succeed can make us sick. Disease-causing invaders are called pathogens and include viruses and "unfriendly" bacteria. Unluckily for them, our bodies have a super-strong defense system. Any pathogens that manage to get in face a deadly army of defenders. Without this army we wouldn't last very long! The body's defenses are known as the immune system.

Plenty of viruses and bacteria try to get

into the blood through food, so it's the role of the liver to filter the blood for anything that shouldn't be there. The liver is where all the nutrients from the food get taken from the blood and properly processed. The dark red, wedge-shaped liver weighs just over three pounds. It is like a huge factory and has over 250 jobs to do. It takes the nutrients, turns them into anything the body needs, and then sends them to the right places as part of the digestive system. While it does this, the liver also cleans and filters the blood.

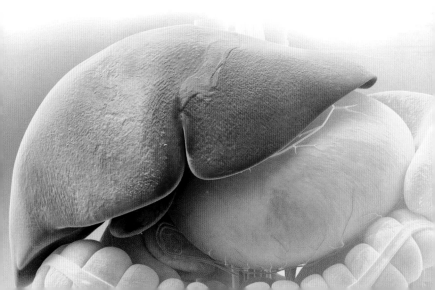

The liver is made up of many different sections, called lobules, that make sure no blood cell is missed. Each section filters the blood again and again, and collects every last bit of nutrients, and destroys any toxins, pathogens, and unwanted waste. The blood passes through the fronds and frills of the

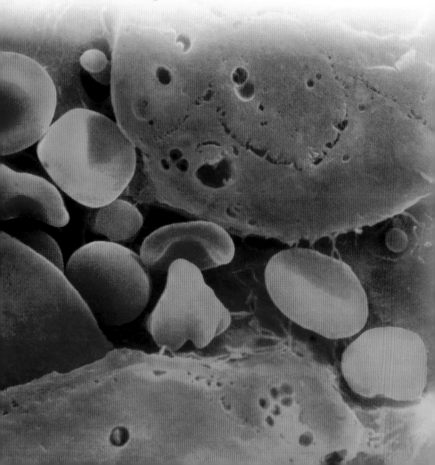

lobules like fish through seaweed. The liver releases heat from this process, keeping the body warm.

Even if the viruses and bacteria do get through the liver's cleaning system, all the white blood cells in the area are alerted. White blood cells are found in the blood all around the body, as well as collecting in specific areas where attack is most likely as a first line of defense.

Many infections enter the body through the air we breathe. The common cold is an infection we may get frequently. When someone coughs or sneezes, the virus sprays out and could land on cells in the nose and throat. At the back of the mouth are several patches of tissue called tonsils. They are full of white blood cells that fight germs in the throat. Sometimes, the tonsils fill with germs themselves and that's when they have to be removed by a doctor.

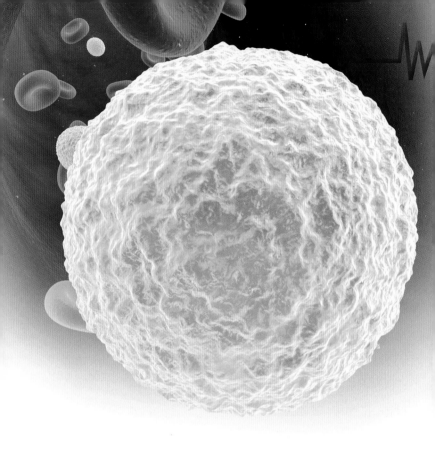

There are different types of white blood cells, which attack in waves. At the first sign of invasion by pathogens, white cells called phagocytes rush to the site, find the germs, and gobble them up. White blood cells called macrophages are a type of phagocyte. They kill germs by swallowing them. When a macrophage finds a germ, it stretches out, wraps around the germ, and pulls it inside. Digestive juices inside the cell then destroy the germ.

If the virus still survives, then the white blood cells called lymphocytes rush in. These long-lived cells keep a record of all the pathogens that have gotten into the body. If a pathogen shows up again, lymphocytes release a killer substance called an antibody, which targets that specific pathogen. The antibody sticks to the surface of the pathogen, preventing it from working and telling other white blood cells to attack and destroy it. Some white blood cells destroy the infected cells, and the phagocytes swallow up anything remaining of the virus. Our bodies get hotter when fighting germs, which gives us a high temperature (a fever).

?

What is an antibody?

Doctors can prevent people from getting a particular disease by injecting a vaccine into their body. A vaccine contains a weak or dead version of the pathogen. This makes the immune system produce antibodies but doesn't cause any illness. If the real pathogen then turns up, it gets wiped out by the army of antibodies that's already waiting there.

In the end, though, looking after our bodies is best of all. A fit body is more likely to be healthy and last longer. Unfortunately, compared to our ancient ancestors, who were forever chasing after antelopes or

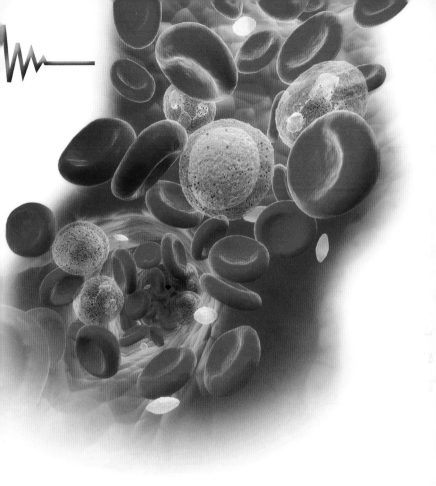

running away from lions, our modern lifestyle tends to involve much more sitting around, playing with computers, watching television, and eating junk food. So, to keep our bodies fit, we need daily exercise and a mixed diet that includes plenty of fruit and vegetables and not too much fat.

Disease Destroyers

Help! The human body is being attacked! Have a look at the white blood cells below. Each cell has its own special function to keep the body safe from germs and infections. Identify the danger and choose the right one to save the body.

Join the Immunity Army!
It's bacteria-bashing time!

The Scavengers

Monocyte

Monocytes patrol the tissues in the body in search of intruders. They are able to kill infected host cells that bacteria have attached to, in order to stop them from spreading throughout the body.

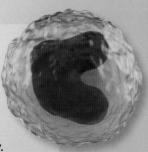

Defender Cells

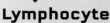

↓

Lymphocyte

Lymphocytes produce antibodies when they come into contact with a harmful cell. Antibodies are proteins that destroy invading foreign cells.

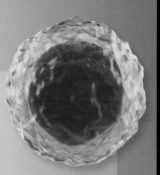

Attack Cells

↓

Neutrophil

Neutrophils patrol the bloodstream and "eat" any attacking organisms. Once the neutrophil has deactivated the intruder, it will also die, making the infected area safe.

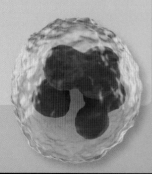

The Commander

⌐➔

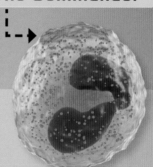

Eosinophil

Eosinophils are in charge! They regulate the body's response to parasites and allergens. When they meet invading organisms, they release chemicals that destroy the virus.

Virus Outbreak Notice

This is an example of an outbreak notice:
THE AGENCY OF HEALTH PROTECTION urges
citizens to take steps in order to prevent a further
outbreak of a new airborne virus that has been
sweeping the nation. The disease contains an
allergen that can cause an eczema-like rash if it
comes into contact with human skin. An official
effort to minimize the spread has been started.

How is the virus spread?

The virus is spread from one person to the next in
a similar way as the common cold is.

The virus is carried within the respiratory system and
is transferred by tiny droplets of mucus (snot).

What are the symptoms?

Itchy red rashes appear on the skin. The rash starts
in a small area and then will spread if not treated.

What should I do if I think I have contracted the virus?

If the rash does not disappear after 3 days, seek
advice from your doctor, who will be able to prescribe
an ointment to soothe the affected area.

Five Steps to Reduce Risk

Please take the following steps in order to keep yourself and those close to you at minimal risk:

1 Avoid contact with those who could be infected. If you think you have contracted the virus yourself, then stay home until symptoms have been gone for at least 24 hours.

2 Wash your hands after covering your nose and mouth when sneezing.

3 Clean surfaces regularly because germs can also spread this way. Computer keyboards, phones, doorknobs, and pens can also hold germs.

4 Stay strong and healthy. Get plenty of sleep and eat lots of fruit and vegetables. This will help keep your immune system in good condition.

5 Avoid touching your face, especially your eyes, nose, and mouth, after touching surfaces in a public area.

History of Medical Pioneers

2600 BCE Chinese emperor **Huang Ti** lays down the basic principles of Chinese medicine.

1543 Flemish doctor **Andreas Vesalius** publishes the first accurate description of human anatomy in his book *On the Structure of the Human Body*.

1818 British doctor **James Blundell** performs the first successful transfusion of human blood to a human patient.

2000 BCE   **1500**   **1700**   **1800**

1796 British doctor **Edward Jenner** performs a vaccination against smallpox by inoculating a child with a vaccine containing the weaker cowpox virus.

1846 American dentist **William Morton** uses ether as a general anesthetic to make a patient unconscious and pain-free during an operation.

It has taken humans thousands of years to learn how to combat diseases. Each breakthrough has helped save lives, and new treatments are still being discovered today.

1895 German physicist **Wilhelm Roentgen** discovers X-rays.

1928 British doctor **Alexander Fleming** discovers penicillin, a substance released by mold that kills bacteria. It will later become the first antibiotic.

1965 British scientist **Harold Hopkins** produces a sophisticated endoscope that gives doctors a clear view of tissues inside the body.

1900

1898 French physicists **Marie** and **Pierre Curie** discover the radioactive element radium, later used in the treatment of cancers.

1967 South African surgeon **Christiaan Barnard** carries out the first successful heart transplant.

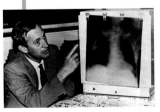

75

Chapter 5
Scaling the Skeletal System

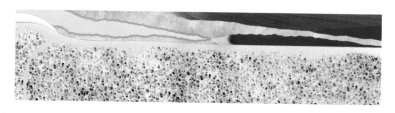

Did you know that our bodies have 206 bones? Some of them are tiny, like the rice grain-sized stirrup bone deep inside the ear. Others, like the mighty femur in the thigh, are big and strong enough to carry our weight. Without the supporting skeleton, the body would be as useful as a tent without poles. Inside the flexible but strong bony framework, soft organs like the brain and heart are protected from damage. Bones also provide somewhere to anchor muscles, so that we can do things and move around.

From the outside, bones may feel hard and look uninteresting, but inside bones are made up of fascinating layers of different bits. The outer layer of bone has tubes of bony tissue running along it—like rolled-up newspaper—that give the bone strength. These tubes are crammed together and so are called compact bone. Once inside these extremely tough walls, toward the center, bone becomes spongy. If bones weren't spongy, they would be too heavy to move.

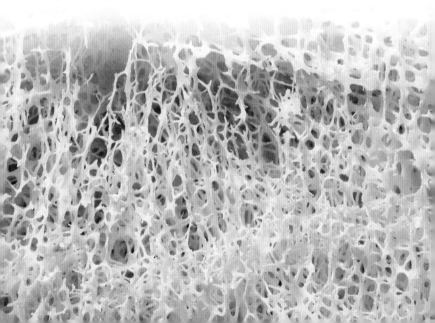

Spindles crisscross throughout the entire area, overlapping and intersecting. A complex, honeycomb structure connects every part of the solid walls to each other. The walls and pillarlike spindles are a gray-white color. These allow the bones to be hollow, while still extra strong.

They are hollow because the insides of our bones are filled with soft jellylike tissue called bone marrow. There are two types of

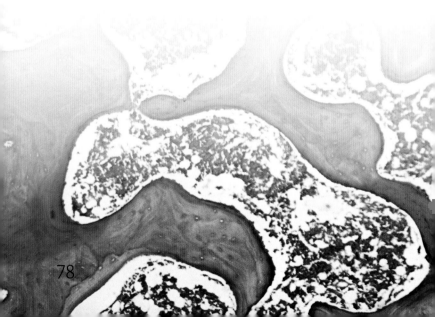

bone marrow named for their colors: red and yellow. Yellow bone marrow stores fat. Red bone marrow makes blood cells.

One of the many jobs of bones, besides supporting our weight and keeping us protected, is to house our blood factories. It is here where the red blood cells and white blood cells are made. Red marrow is found inside the flatter bones—shoulder blades, ribs, breastbone, and pelvis.

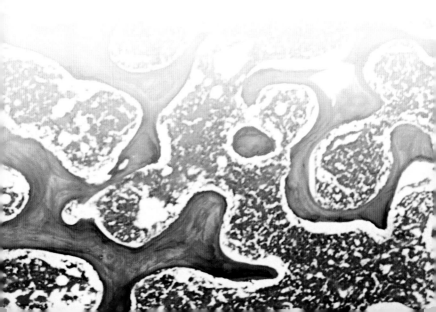

The high-speed red marrow production line churns out exactly the right number of red blood cells needed to replace the worn-out ones. A large canal of thick liquid thrives with red blood cells, which float up and out toward the large veins in the bones. More cells take their place behind...and more...and still more. It seems endless. The blood cells swarm around—two million of them being produced every second. Among them white blood cells cruise pass, patrolling for anything amiss.

Living bones are therefore nothing like the dry, dusty, dead ones we see from old skeletons dug up. They are one-third water, full of nerves and blood vessels, and contain cells that are forever rebuilding and reshaping our bones. They are made of mineral salts for hardness and collagen fibers for strength. After death, the collagen rots away leaving just a hard but brittle bone-shaped shell.

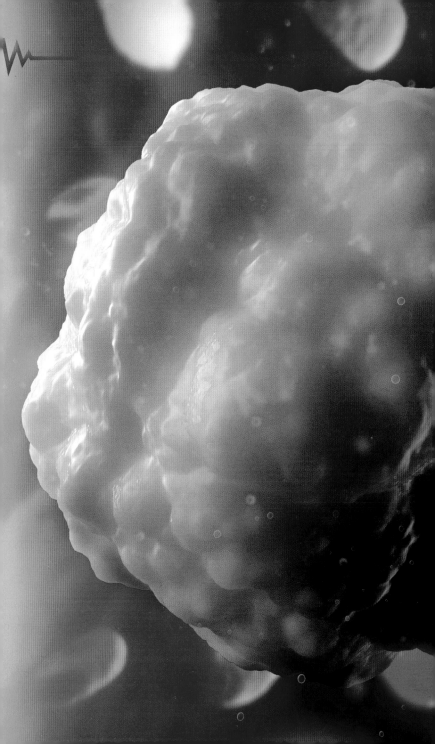

When we were much younger and smaller, we started out with many more bones then we have now. A newborn baby has more than 300 "bones" making up its skeleton. Some of these "bones" are not very hard though. They are made of cartilage, the stuff that makes the nose and ear flexible. Then as we get older, real bone replaces cartilage to make the bones longer and stronger, and some bones join together.

Bones are connected by joints, which make movement possible. Some joints, like those in the hip and shoulder, allow all-around movement. Others, like the hinge joint in the knee, only allow movement back and forth. To stop lots of grinding noises when we move, most joints have thick, oily liquid inside, which makes them work smoothly, like a well-oiled machine.

While joints are great for making the skeleton flexible, without ligaments they would be useless. Ligaments are strong, slightly stretchy straps that hold bones together at the joints, like in the knee. They stop bones from moving too much or in the wrong directions. Sometimes, people push their bones too far. The bones pop out of their joints and tear the ligaments. Doctors call this dislocation and it needs expert skills to carefully maneuver the bones back into place without too much nerve pinching or tissue crunching. Ouch!

?

Why do adults have fewer bones than a newborn baby?

Blood Factory

Red blood cells are worn out after about 120 days so the body is in need of a constant supply of new ones. Millions of new cells enter the bloodstream from the bone marrow every minute.

1 The kidneys send out signals to the red bone marrow telling it to start the cogs turning and make new red blood cells.

2 The machine starts to whir and the production line starts.

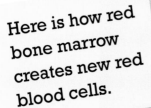

Here is how red bone marrow creates new red blood cells.

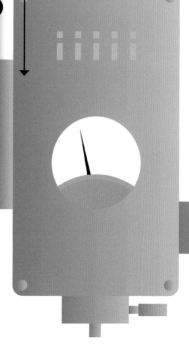

Blood cell production line

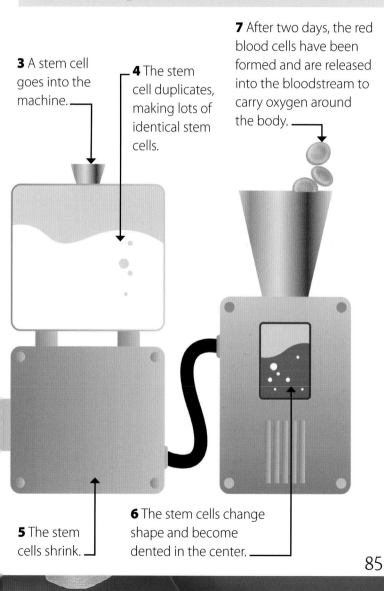

3 A stem cell goes into the machine.

4 The stem cell duplicates, making lots of identical stem cells.

7 After two days, the red blood cells have been formed and are released into the bloodstream to carry oxygen around the body.

5 The stem cells shrink.

6 The stem cells change shape and become dented in the center.

Skeleton Dance

The following song is based on an old spiritual song *Dem Bones* by the songwriter James Weldon Johnson (1871–1938). Dance along as you say or sing the words, pointing to the various bones.

The toe bone's connected to the foot bone,
The foot bone's connected to the ankle bone,
The ankle bone's connected to the leg bone,
Let's shake those bones about!
The leg bone's connected to the knee bone,
The knee bone's connected to the thigh bone,
The thigh bone's connected to the hip bone,
Let's shake those bones about!
The hip bone's connected to the back bone
The back bone's connected to the neck bone,
The neck bone's connected to the head bone,
Let's shake those bones about!
Them bones, them bones, them dry bones.
Them bones, them bones, them dry bones.
Them bones, them bones, them dry bones.
Let's shake those bones about!

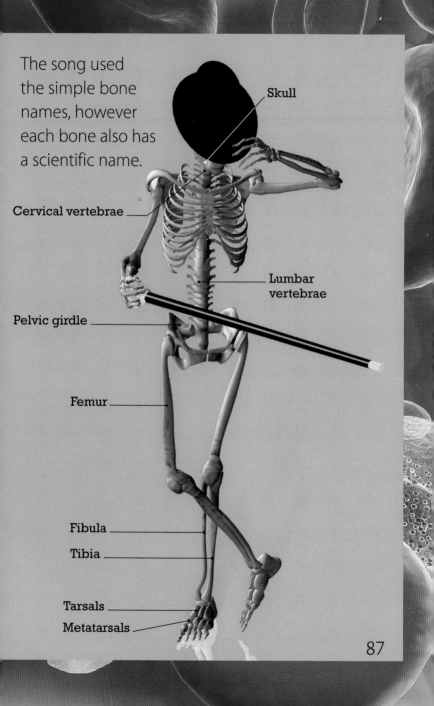

The song used the simple bone names, however each bone also has a scientific name.

Skull

Cervical vertebrae

Lumbar vertebrae

Pelvic girdle

Femur

Fibula

Tibia

Tarsals

Metatarsals

87

"Doctor, Doctor" Jokes

"Doctor, Doctor" jokes have been around for hundreds of years. Some researchers found some in the world's oldest surviving joke book from the third century. So they date back to at least ancient Roman times.

Doctor, Doctor, I've broken my arm in two places.

Well, don't go back there again then!

Doctor, Doctor, you have to help me out!

Certainly! Which way did you come in?

Doctor, Doctor, I keep thinking there are two of me.

One at a time, please.

Doctor, Doctor, I think I'm a telephone.

Well, take these pills and if they don't work, then give me a ring!

Doctor, Doctor, I've swallowed my pocket money.

Take this and we'll see if there's any change in the morning.

Doctor, Doctor, I feel like a pair of curtains.

Well, pull yourself together then.

Doctor, Doctor, I dream there are monsters under my bed. What can I do?

Saw the legs off your bed!

Doctor, Doctor, I think I'm a bridge.

What's come over you?

Oh! Two cars, a large truck, and a coach.

Doctor, Doctor, I'm becoming invisible.

Yes, I can see you're not all there!

Doctor, Doctor, I keep thinking I'm a caterpillar.

Don't worry! You'll soon change!

Chapter 6
Must be the Muscular System

Do you know what surrounds almost every bone in the body? Muscles. To work properly, bones need muscles. Hundreds of skeletal muscles pull on our bones so we can walk, write, and do thousands of other things.

To imagine what muscles look like, take a trip to the meat counter at the local supermarket—vegetarians beware! Those red chunks of meat are the skeletal muscles of sheep, cows, and other animals. The "meat" from our bodies makes up more than 40 percent of our body weight.

Muscles move all the time, even in just tiny ways we don't even notice. Since muscles need to be so flexible, so do their blood vessels. There are tiny tunnels with uncountable alleys and offshoots of other blood vessels all around. Oxygen is extremely important for muscles, so they need blood to get to them at all times. We wouldn't want to lose blood because the muscle cut it off by moving. The blood vessels need to move with the muscles, like rocking on the sea.

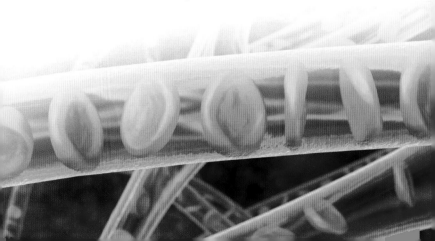

There are 640 muscles around the skeleton alone, but most of those muscles don't work alone. They work together in groups to pull different ways and allow the body to carefully adjust into position.

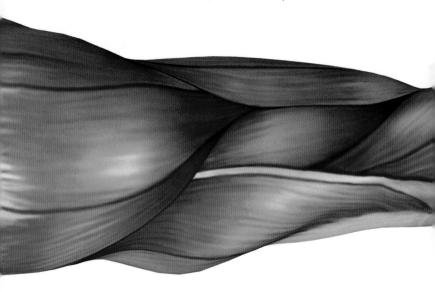

Pulling may be a speciality of muscles, but pushing certainly isn't. Each one can only move one way, so they need to work as a team. Although we can move our arms in lots of different ways, like when we move them up and down, muscles can only contract (get shorter)! They just all do it in different directions. So when one muscle pulls the arm up, another one pulls it back again to lower it.

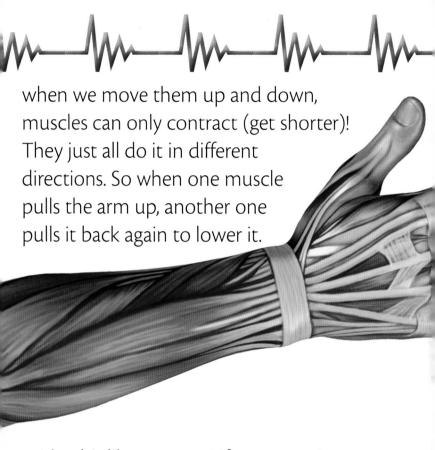

It's a bit like a seesaw! If a person sits on one end, that side goes down but can't go up. Only if they work with someone on the other end, can they then make each other go up and down.

This arrangement of muscles is found all over the body. Some pull bones one way, and others pull in the opposite direction.

Muscles also need to be able to stretch. When we exercise our muscles or lift heavy things, knowing how they work and what they are made from will help us. If a person strains a muscle more than it's used to, the muscle can tear. Thankfully the body is very adaptive. If someone tears their muscles, the body will repair them, but—and this is amazing—it will repair them to be stronger than before.

How? Muscles are made of hundreds of thousands of tiny fibers, all wrapped up together like a bale of hay. These are long and packed with special stringy threads. So when a muscle is used a lot or damaged, the old fibers are repaired and some more muscle fibers are wrapped around the damage to make that particular place stronger. Our bodies want to make us as durable as we need to be. If people

do a lot of the same activity, like a runner training for the Olympics, the muscles they are using are made stronger so they can do it more easily.

?

How do muscles repair themselves and get stronger?

The threads in each fiber of a muscle also work together. These are what make each muscle fiber contract. When the brain sends a signal to a muscle, the fibers in the muscle contract, the whole muscle gets shorter, and that part of the body moves.

A tough cord called a tendon links the muscles to the bones. Over 20 muscles in the forearm pull on the long tendons in hand bones to make hundreds of different types of movements, from a powerful grip to the most delicate touch.

Face muscles are a bit unusual because instead of pulling on bones, they tug at the skin on the face. Just a tiny twitch can alter our facial expression to reveal a subtle change in mood. In fact, it is almost impossible to hide our feelings from being expressed on our faces.

A number of muscles work all the time we are awake. Those in the back, neck, and

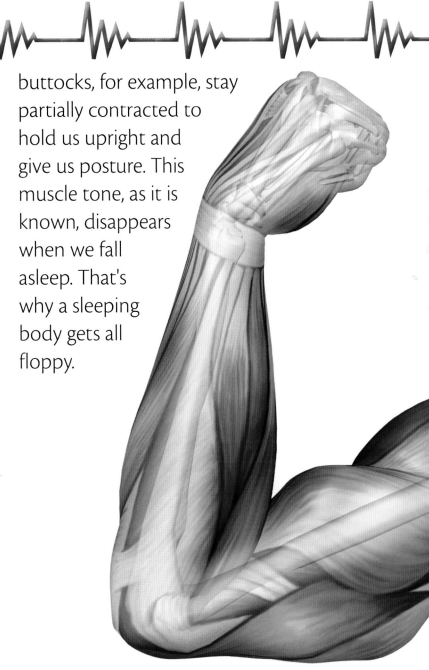

buttocks, for example, stay partially contracted to hold us upright and give us posture. This muscle tone, as it is known, disappears when we fall asleep. That's why a sleeping body gets all floppy.

Muscle Machine

All muscles in the human body have to work together to keep us on the move. Even the smallest muscles have their own part to play.

Components

About 640 muscles cover a human skeleton. Most are connected to the bones with stretchy straps of tendons.

Smooth muscle forms part of organs. These muscles are made of long, thin fibers and are mostly linked together in muscular sheets.

Hip muscles

Quadriceps

Hamstring muscle

Wow!
The fastest muscles are in your eyeballs, shifting your gaze in 0.02 of a second!

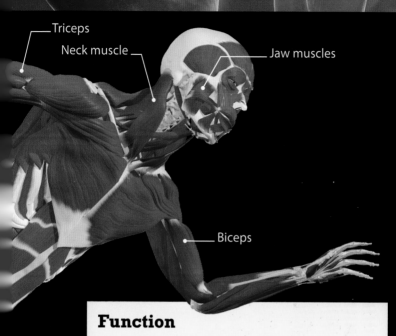

Triceps

Neck muscle

Jaw muscles

Biceps

Function

■ Skeletal muscles shrink and shorten to pull tight and move bones. You can purposely control these via neurons in the nerves from your brain.

Main features

■ The biggest muscles pull your legs straight at the hip.

■ The smallest muscles are inside your ear.

■ There are more than 14 muscles in your tongue.

■ Calf muscles pull your heels so you can walk, run, or stand on tiptoe.

Funny Faces

This diagram shows some of the main muscles that make facial expressions.

There are more than 40 muscles in your face that can make over 7,000 different expressions. A slight muscle pull can make tiny, precise movements of the facial skin.

Flat forehead muscle raises the eyebrow and wrinkles the forehead.

Circular eye muscle helps close the eyelid.

Cheek muscle pulls corner of the mouth upward and outward.

Mouth muscle brings lips together and helps shape words when speaking.

Jaw muscle pulls corner of mouth outward.

Lower jaw muscle pulls corner of mouth downward.

How many funny faces can you make? Which muscles are you moving?

Clench test

1 Hold your hand above your head and clench and unclench your fist. Count how many times you can clench it before it starts feeling uncomfortable.

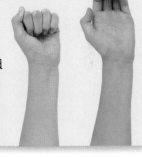

2 Now do the same with your other hand, but this time hold it down by your side. How many times can you clench before this feels uncomfortable?

Relax test

Clasp your hands together with the fingers interlocked. Stretch out your index fingers straight and parallel to each other so they are not touching.

What happens to your index fingers when you let your arm muscles relax?

Explanation of test results

You should manage more clenches with your hand held by your side. This is because blood flows more quickly downward than upward, since the oxygen supply reaches the muscles quicker.

Your fingers should move toward each other as they relax. This is because skeletal muscles return to a relaxed position when not active.

Chapter 7
Navigating the Nervous System

At this second, billions of microscopic nerve cells are sending a stream of electrical signals to our brains and back again. The soft, wrinkly, walnut-shaped brain is the control center that is responsible for our personalities, intelligence, powers of communication, imagination, and controlling most of the body activities. The nerve cells called neurons make up the nervous system.

The nervous system is like our bodies' wiring. The brain sends signals to every part of the body at once, telling which systems to operate and when, with intricate details. That makes the whole body like some kind of computer. If the body is like a computer, then it's one of the most powerful in existence. Even in this modern day, our technology is still catching up with nature.

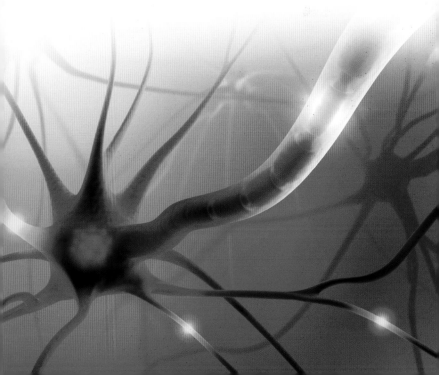

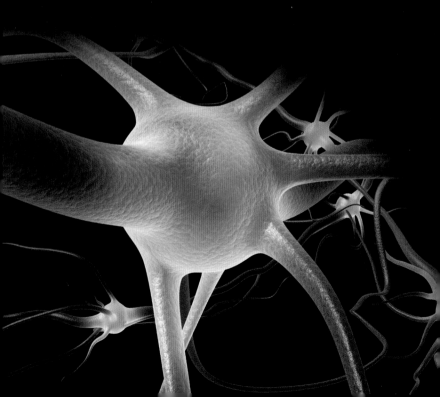

Neurons are slightly different from other body cells because they specialize in carrying electrical signals called nerve impulses at very high speed. Each one of these neurons has connections with hundreds or even thousands of other neurons that together produce a massive network. This receives messages from sensors, for example from inside the eye so we can see where we're going. The network sends out instructions, so we can do things like walk in a straight line. The network also analyzes and stores information so we think and remember.

The brain links to the rest of the body via the spinal cord and nerves. Finger-thick and squashy, the spinal cord runs through the backbone and relays messages to and from the brain. Nerves pop out of the spinal cord, and then branch out to carry nerve impulses to and from all parts of the body. The spinal cord is also responsible for split-second responses called reflexes that protect us from everyday hazards. If we catch a finger on a cactus, then a nerve impulse zooms up to the spinal cord, and—without having to think about it—straight back to an arm muscle that immediately pulls the hand away.

Every little fiber in each muscle is made of nerve endings, acting like an on-off switch. When the brain needs a muscle to work, it sends a message to this nerve bundle, and it'll contract itself. When the

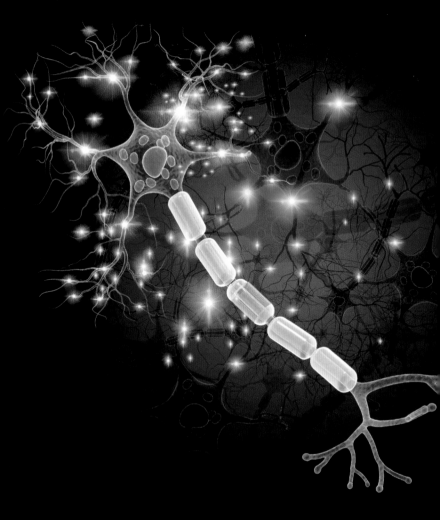

muscle is damaged, the brain will get
a message from here, letting it know.
It's like its own little two-way radio.

A neuron is so small for something
so important. All nerve endings are
microscopic, since they wind their way
through every tiny bit of the body.
Neurons are so small and quick that they
can travel from the brain to the big toe in
just 0.01 second.

Having a brain wave usually means that
we've had a brilliant idea. But the brain
actually gives off brain waves all the time,
day and night. These are produced by
the billions of electrical signals that flash
between over 100 billion neurons in the
brain every second. Brain waves vary
depending on whether we are resting,
really concentrating, or sleeping at the
back of the class.

The brain is the hub of everything. The main section is the big wrinkly bit called the cerebrum. The cerebrum is divided into two halves called the left and right cerebral hemispheres. The left hemisphere controls the right side of the body, and the right hemisphere the left side. Usually the left hemisphere is dominant, which makes most people right-handed. The left hemisphere also controls speech, writing, numbers, and problem solving, while the right hemisphere deals with art, music, and recognizing faces.

The connections between all those billions of brain cells are responsible for our intelligence. We might think men are more intelligent than women, because an average man's brain weighs three pounds and a woman's weighs slightly less. However, intelligence does not depend on brain size, but on the number of connections between

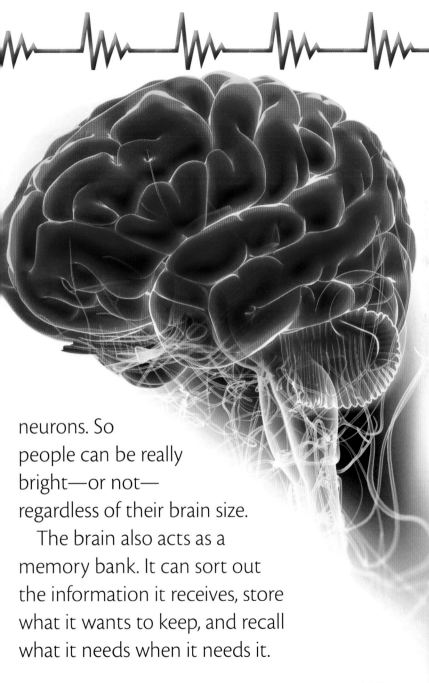

neurons. So
people can be really
bright—or not—
regardless of their brain size.

The brain also acts as a
memory bank. It can sort out
the information it receives, store
what it wants to keep, and recall
what it needs when it needs it.

When we are wide awake, our versatile brains let us communicate with each other. The way most humans do this is by speaking a common language. We think about what we want to say, and a part of the left half of the brain sends instructions to the vocal cords in the throat so that we make sounds. But there are other ways of getting feelings across. Gestures and body language—the way the body is positioned when talking or listening to people—are both important.

Life would also be dull without our imaginations. Most conscious creative thoughts and ideas come from the right half of the brain. But imagination can also involve unconscious thoughts. These come from deep inside the brain where our basic emotions also arise.

When we sleep, scientists think this gives the brain time to sort out the previous day's experiences, and gives the body a chance to rest. Sleeping and waking are part of a natural 24-hour rhythm also controlled by the brain. Our bodies just can't survive without it.

Gray Matters

Using Your Head

The brain is made from cells that do all of your thinking and feeling. Different areas of the brain control different bodily functions including thinking, moving, feeling, and memory.

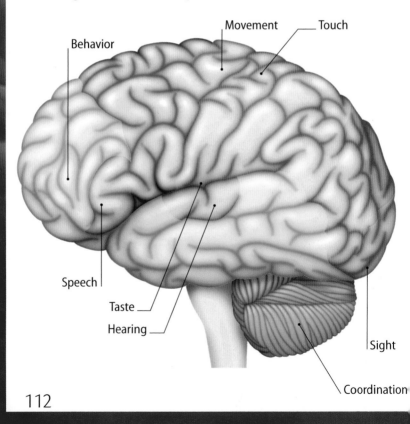

Behavior

Movement

Touch

Speech

Taste

Hearing

Sight

Coordination

Why do we need a brain?

Here are examples of just some of the activities that we need our brain for.

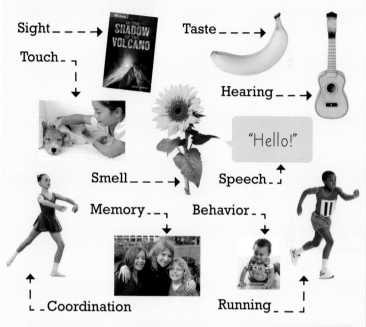

Sight - - - →

Touch

Taste - - - →

Hearing - - →

"Hello!"

Smell - - - →

Speech

Memory

Behavior

Coordination

Running

Are You a Genius?

An IQ (intelligence quotient) test measures intelligence but this can mean many different things. Discover which aspect you are best at by taking this genius test.

Spatial intelligence

1. Which shape completes the sentence?

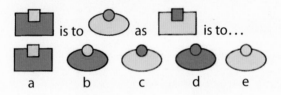

is to   as   is to...

a   b   c   d   e

Verbal intelligence

2. Which word doesn't belong?
a) shout
b) sing
c) talk
d) walk
e) whisper

Numerical intelligence

3. 1985516 is to sheep as 2315126 is to

a) wolf

b) horse

c) antelope

d) goat

e) cattle

Hint:
a=1, b=2, c=3... z=26

Lateral thinking

4. It's spring. You see a carrot and two pieces of coal together in somebody's front garden. How did they get there?

5. A man lives on the tenth floor of a building. Every day he takes the elevator to the ground floor to go to work. When he returns, he takes the elevator to the seventh floor and walks the rest of the way. If it's raining, he takes the elevator all the way up. Why?
Clue: *he owns an umbrella.*

Navigating the Nervous System

Your mission, Agent Neuron, should you choose to accept it, is to deliver a top-secret message to the right hand in a split second. Our superiors in the brain have informed us that this hand has touched something hot. We need to move this hand away from the heat as soon as possible in order to eliminate any risk to our human. A map of the nervous system showing the brain, spinal cord, and all the nerves is pictured here; this specifies the route you need to take. Beware of any danger along the way and good luck, Agent Neuron! We're counting on you.

Nerves
THE ROUTE NETWORK
Bundles of fibers that spread all over the body. These carry signals between the brain and other parts of the body.

Neuron
THE AGENT
One of billions of nerve cells that use electrical and chemical signals to process and send information, telling the body what to do, for example move a finger.

Brain
THE CONTROL CENTER
A central web of thick wrinkles of folded tissue where instructions are received, interpreted, and sent out.

Nervous system map

This system regulates almost every bodily process—from breathing to controlling reactions when feeling physical pain.

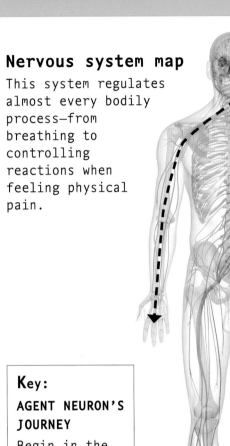

Key:

AGENT NEURON'S JOURNEY

Begin in the brain, travel down the spine, and then along to the right hand.

Epilogue
A World Inside Us All

Look down at your hands. Imagine the blood cells, the bones all connected, the network of nerves running throughout, all working together.

Wriggle your fingers. Be aware of the muscles in your arms pulling on the tendons to make the bones move, with the brain commanding the movement.

Make a fist and examine the blood vessels. Know that they are filled with blood on an amazing journey, being continually pumped around the body by the heart, transferring oxygen and other treats to all parts.

Examine your hand for cuts. Be impressed how the platelets help mend them and the white blood cells keep your body healthy.

All this is going on inside all of us at this very moment. Wow!

A Trip Through the Body Quiz

See if you can remember the answers to these questions about what you have read.

1. What is an endoscope?

2. What makes blood red?

3. What is the function of white blood cells?

4. Why might a person find it difficult to breathe?

5. How does the body stop food from going into the windpipe?

6. What are the feelers in the small intestine connected to?

7. Where in the body would you expect to find proteases?

8. What does the liver do to the blood?

9. Who carried out the first successful heart transplant?

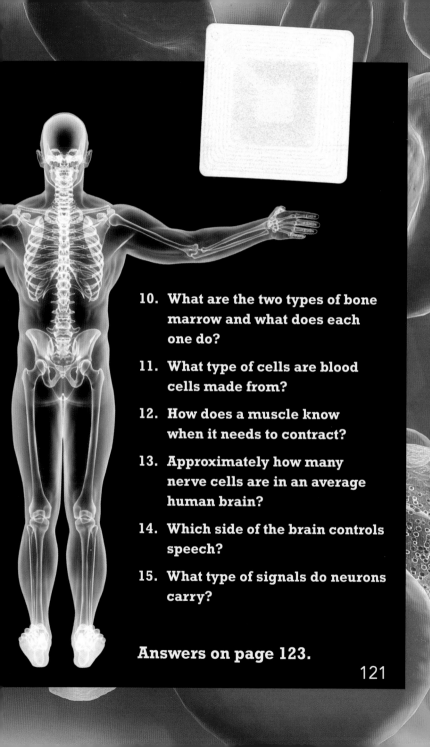

10. What are the two types of bone marrow and what does each one do?

11. What type of cells are blood cells made from?

12. How does a muscle know when it needs to contract?

13. Approximately how many nerve cells are in an average human brain?

14. Which side of the brain controls speech?

15. What type of signals do neurons carry?

Answers on page 123.

Glossary

Antibody
A substance made by the body that sticks to germs and marks them for destruction by white blood cells.

Artery
A blood vessel that carries blood away from the heart to the body's tissues and organs.

Blood vessel
A tube that carries blood through the body.

Capillary
The smallest type of blood vessel.

Cells
The smallest living units that are the building blocks of the human body.

Digestion
The process that breaks down food into tiny particles that your body can absorb and use.

Hemoglobin
Substance that carries oxygen in red blood cells.

Immune system
A collection of cells and tissues that protect the body from disease by searching for and destroying germs.

Mucus
A slippery liquid that lines the respiratory and digestive systems.

Nerve
Cablelike bundle of neurons that links all body parts to the brain and spinal cord.

Neuron
A nerve cell that carries information around the body as electrical signals.

Organ
Major body part that has a specific function within the body, such as the heart or brain.

Plasma
The liquid, colorless part of the blood.

Vein
A blood vessel that carries blood toward the heart.

Villi
Tiny fingerlike projections from the small intestine wall that transfer nutrients into the bloodstream.

Answers to A Trip Through the Body Quiz:
1. A small instrument, often a camera, which doctors use to look inside patients' bodies; **2.** Hemoglobin—a red-colored protein contained in red blood cells; **3.** Patrol the bloodstream and fight off diseases and infections; **4.** Because they have asthma; **5.** The epiglottis moves to cover the windpipe when we eat; **6.** The bloodstream; **7.** In the stomach; **8.** Filters and cleans; **9.** Christiaan Barnard; **10.** Yellow bone marrow stores fat, red bone marrow makes blood cells; **11.** Stem cells; **12.** The brain sends a message to the nerve cells in the muscle; **13.** 100 billion; **14.** Left cerebral hemisphere; **15.** Electrical.

Index

About the Author

Laurie Blake comes from London, England, where he read and wrote stories until he was old enough to call it his job. He likes inline skating, eating tomatoes, and learning Japanese despite his dyslexia. Sometimes he combines these things, but it often ends up getting messy! His main superpowers include being able to improvise stories at any time, reel off an almost endless number of puns, and completely forget what he went to the store for in the first place.

About the Consultants

Dr. Linda Gambrell, Distinguished Professor of Education at Clemson University, has served as President of the National Reading Conference, the College Reading Association, and the International Reading Association. She is also reading consultant for the *DK Readers*.

Steve Parker earned his bachelor of science degree in Zoology with highest honors. He is a Senior Scientific Fellow of the Zoological Society of London. He has written more than 70 books on the human body for a variety of readerships, from youngsters starting school to university students of medicine and allied sciences. His titles include the international best-selling *The Human Body Book* (DK, revised 2013) and the new *Superhuman* (DK, 2014) with Robert Winston. His most recent title in the medical area is *Kill or Cure: An Illustrated History of Medicine* (DK, 2013).

OVERBROOK PARK

Have you read these other great books from DK?

III DK ADVENTURES **III**

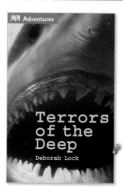

Discover the wonders of the world's deepest, darkest ocean trench.

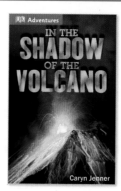

Mount Vesuvius erupts in this adventure. Will Carlo escape?

It's a life-or-death adventure as the gang searches for a new home planet.

Chase twisters in Tornado Alley in this pulse-racing action adventure.

Discover what life for pilots, women, and children was like during WWII.

Emma adores horses. Will her wish come true at a riding camp?

126